How to Book of Effective Meetings

Author
J H Hood

ISBN
978-0-9875575-2-0

Dedication

To all those people who have and are still walking the learning journey with me—thank you a thousand times over.

May we continue the journey with joy in the challenges.

Contents

The elements of a successful meeting

Meetings—in one form or another—are a constant in many people's lives. We have all experienced meetings that are frustrating, time consuming or just plain confusing.

They don't have to be like that!

Most meetings can be enjoyable and productive, if you get some basic things right.

These success factors are:
- understanding **the reason** for the meeting, and what you want to achieve from it
- having all members of the meeting **understanding their role and the role of others**, including the Chairperson, the Executive Officer and <u>every</u> participant
- getting the **arrangements right:** when, where, resources, etc
- setting and using an **agenda**
- taking and using **minutes** effectively

- recognizing the **time wasters**
- dealing with the **interactions** between participants
- understanding the **value of differences** and how to manage conflict

In this tool we explore each of these elements.

Using the checklists

There are **checklists** included at the end of this tool. They are a distillation of many years of practice in setting up, chairing and participating in meetings. They are a powerful means of improving your meeting skill—**if you use them regularly**.

The **checklists** are designed to be used in a range of ways:
- when setting up a meeting
- when choosing a Chairperson
- for taking minutes
- for understanding the roles of all the participants
- as a means of reviewing the progress of your meetings over a period of time
- as a refresher for you in the conduct of the meeting
- to help manage conflict, and to better understand people's behavior
- to assess your meeting processes

Checklist 1—**Why hold this meeting?**

Why is this meeting being held?

A good meeting brings the right people together, for a clearly understood reason, and results in either a **decision** or effective **sharing of information**. It is a means of:
- exchanging information
- keeping communication channels open
- making decisions
- addressing issues
- building solutions

It is important to ask, 'Why are we having this meeting? Is there another way? Is it the most cost effective way? What would happen if we didn't hold the meeting?'

Don't hold a meeting if:
- the information can be shared in another way, e.g. memo, newsletter, email, video, telephone call, etc
- the person with the authority to make the decision would not be at the meeting
- the problem can be solved in another way
- key people or information are not available
- the costs of calling the meeting are higher than the value of the decision or information. And

don't forget to include the value of people's time!

Especially, **don't hold a meeting** if *'We've always had one in the past'*, or *'They always go over time'*, or *'Nothing happens as a result of the meeting'*. These are **warning signs** that maybe the meeting is not needed, and certainly that it could be managed differently.

Not sure you need a meeting? Use:

Checklist 1—Why hold this meeting?

Formal and informal meetings

There are two types of meetings: **formal** and **informal**.

Formal meetings are those that have set rules and procedures, and official agendas and minutes. The requirements may vary according to national or local legal requirements, or the constitution or structure of the body or organization.
Formal meetings are normally be meetings such as an annual general meeting of a company or association, a local government council meeting, or a formally composed committee meeting or standing committee.

You will need to investigate the specific rules and procedures for these meetings, and follow them. **However, you will find that applying our checklists and suggestions will also improve the conduct of your formal meetings.**

Informal meetings make up the vast majority of meetings that we attend. They may be casual, normally don't have formal rules of procedure and sometimes have no written minutes or—in the worst case—no agenda.

However, just because the style of the meeting may be informal, **it does not mean** that it should be conducted without preparation, without some agreed procedures and behaviors, or without clear lines of responsibility and accountability. And, **every** meeting should have an agenda!

It is also important to understand that an informal meeting can be either an **information meeting** or a **decision making meeting**.

The focus of **an information meeting is on advising, updating or selling**. The emphasis is on content, the meeting is often one way and there are usually many people in attendance.

> The focus of a **decision-making meeting is goal setting, problem solving, and setting directions**. The emphasis is on process, problem solving and decision making. The

meetings are interactive and participative and usually they have 12 or fewer participants.

You need to establish which type of meeting is to be held—each type of meeting needs to be **conducted differently**.

Information Meeting	
Number of attendees	Any number
Who should attend	Those who need to know
Room set up	Participants facing front of room - theatre style
Communication process	One way from leader to participants with opportunities for questions
Most effective style of leadership	Authoritative or directive
Emphasis should be on	Clear and relevant content
Keys to success	Understanding the audience, good preparation and presentation of information

Decision-Making Meeting	
Number of attendees	Small size. Preferably 12 or fewer
Who should attend	Those responsible and who can contribute
Room set up	Participants facing each other—around a table
Communication process	Interactive discussion among all attending
Most effective style of leadership	Participative
Emphasis should be on	Interaction and problem solving
Keys to success	A meeting climate that supports open discussion, well structured agenda, good chairing skills

In the next chapters we highlight potential issues that can arise in any meeting and provide ideas for dealing with them

Timewasters—the Pareto Principle or the 80:20 Rule

The **Pareto Principle**—usually called **the 80:20 Rule**—states that a small number of causes is responsible for a large percentage of the outcomes, in a ratio of about 80:20.

In broad terms, the 80:20 Rule suggests that 80% of your results come from 20% of your activities. When this rule is applied to meetings, it indicates that about **80% of the decisions made in a meeting come from 20% of the meeting time.**

Here are some other examples of the 80:20 Rule:
- 80% of the traffic in town travels over 20% of the roads
- 80% of your profit will come from 20% of your customers

- 80% of your problems will come from 20% of your customers (or staff)
- 80% of the defects will be in 20% of jobs done
- 80% of the outfits you wear come from 20% of the clothes in your wardrobe
- 80% of your call-backs or remedial work will come from 20% of your installation teams

Your meetings will be greatly improved if you are able to **identify and keep discussion focused on**:
- the 20% of your goals, or agenda items, that will contribute to 80% of your effectiveness
- the 80% of a problem which can be solved by identifying and working on the correct 20% of the issues
- when to call a halt to unproductive expenditure of time and energy—when the 80% of benefit which comes from the first 20% of effort has been reached

Most people have sat through a meeting at which 15 or 20 minutes were spent on addressing an item that really could have been dealt with in 2 or 3 minutes And what is worse, only 2 or 3 minutes are then spent on crucial issues!

Using the **80:20 Rule** is a way of identifying priorities and of focusing effort on the items that will bring the **best return on your investment of time and energy.**

Applying the Pareto Principle is an excellent means of improving your meetings.

At the heart of any continuous improvement process are the four steps of **planning, executing, reflecting and learning from past actions**. Reflect on the last two or three meetings you have attended, and ask these questions:

- Which agenda items did we spend most time on?
- What was the outcome from these?
- Was the expenditure of time and energy justified?
- Which agenda items did we get most value from?
- Are there any patterns of behavior or decision making that can be identified?
- What changes could we make at the next meeting?

You might like to invite the participants of your meeting to reflect on these questions—make it an agenda item at your next meeting and distribute the questions with the agenda.

Are you making the most of your meetings? Use:

Checklist 2—Improving meetings

The Agenda

An agenda—whether it is a simple one written five minutes before a meeting, or a more structured one written and distributed well before the meeting—is an **essential element of a good meeting.**

An agenda is:
- a *list or plan* of the things to address during the meeting
- a *means of clarifying* why the meeting is being held, and who should participate
- *information to participants* about the meeting, including what they need to do to prepare for the meeting
- the *'road map'* for the meeting itself
- the main document to which other papers are attached where there is pre–reading required before the meeting

A **good agenda** reminds you to ask these questions:
- Do we have the appropriate people?
- Do we really need this meeting?
- What outcomes do we want from this meeting?

- What information should be provided for participants?
- What venue and facilities does this meeting call for?

An agenda should have sufficient detail to **act as a map or guide, that will show what, when, who and how long** you will talk about each item.

Agenda *items* become the headings for the *minutes* of the meeting.

Wherever possible, the agenda should be sent out **before** the meeting, with any appropriate attachments.

There is an **example** of an **agenda,** and a **blank agenda template** at the end of this eBook.

The value of a good Chairperson

A **good Chairperson** can make the difference between a frustrating and expensive meeting, and one that works well. This doesn't mean that the meeting needs to be very structured or formal, rather that you have a Chairperson **who is able to keep the meeting on track while getting the best out of the participants.**

People become good at chairing meetings through practice, and through using these straightforward tools and hints.

As a good Chairperson, you will:
- be on time
- be prepared—not just in setting and understanding the agenda, but in the content and task requirements
- bring all the necessary papers, or if there is an Executive Officer, make sure they have all the papers
- communicate assertively
- ensure that everyone participates

- encourage respect for all speakers (one voice at a time)
- keep the discussion on the topic
- take notes—not the minutes, just notes to guide the discussion
- be flexible and open to the views of others
- respect confidentiality
- ask for clarification if something is not clear (to you or anyone else)
- be prepared to participate in the discussions
- be prepared to participate in the decision making (according to the agreed role of the chair)
- carry out all of the actions for which you accept responsibility

Determining the agenda is often the task of the Chairperson of the meeting—this will usually be done in consultation with participants and key stakeholders.

The Chairperson is also responsible for determining the **distribution list** of the agenda—again; this may be done in consultation with others, and with the assistance of an Executive Officer if there is one.

The Chairperson should check at the beginning of a meeting for any other agenda items, and manage their inclusion.

An excellent Chairperson:

- **arrives** on time and **starts** on time
- is always looking for **negotiable compromises** and win/win outcomes
- is committed to allowing **fair time** for every one to talk—a balancing act between those who have too much to say, and those who have too little to say
- strives for i**mpartiality**
- doesn't take over the meeting, but is prepared to **direct traffic** where necessary
- is good at **summarizing**—Where have we been? What have we agreed? Where are our differences? Where to from here?
- ensures decisions are made, and actions clearly assigned
-
- If the discussion is becoming too heated or going off track, **stay calm** and try:
- summarizing the issue
- asking a **question**
- **calling** for order
- reminding people to focus on the **issue** not on personalities

- **setting time limits** for speakers—and sticking to them

Use the **power of the group**. Try language like *"We've heard from Lee...what are others' comments on the issue?"*, and then name someone to comment *"What about you, Pat?"* If you can keep the focus on the issues and bring in the rest of the people at the meeting, then you will probably get the meeting back on track.

Sometimes you may have to simply ask the difficult person:*"What is it that is causing you to..."* or *"What is it that we can do to help you move on/clarify/etc ..."* Conflict **not addressed does not go away—it just gets worse!**

If necessary, call for a short break.

If the disruption keeps on, then stop the discussion and suggest that the item be placed on the next meeting's agenda. You may then need to speak with participants before the next meeting—sometimes issues need to be dealt with outside the meeting.

-

- If you can't reach a decision:
- summarize what you <u>do</u> have agreement on
- summarize the <u>issues</u> that are causing difficulties
- ask what other information people may need
- clarify the issues that not making the decision may cause—consequences
- ask whether people need a break

Remember—there are always other options, we just need to discover them!

There are some meetings where the use of an external chairperson will pay very good dividends. The simple criteria to use is *'Will the outcomes of this meeting be enhanced if we use someone who is not affected by the existing dynamics?'* If the answer is yes, then it would be wise to engage an external chairperson.

This is not a reflection on any individual's skills, but rather recognition that there are times when impartial specialist or technical expertise is needed.

Setting up a meeting? Chairing for the first time? Could you improve your chairing performance? Use:

Checklist 3—Chairperson's role

Executive Officer or Executive Secretary or Admin Officer

Many meetings have a person who carries out some of the detailed roles of the Chairperson before and after a meeting, as well as offering support to the Chair during the meeting. This is a valuable role, and performed well can make the difference between a successful and disastrous meeting.

This role often applies when the meeting is one held regularly, possibly with have participants who come from a variety of areas.

The person may be called the **Executive Secretary, or Executive Officer, or Administrative Officer**...the title varies—but the tasks are similar, and may include:
- making the administrative arrangements for the meeting, such as arranging the venue and checking facilities
- distributing the agenda, and any supporting material

- liaising with, and briefing, the Chairperson and other meeting members—often between meetings
- taking and distributing the minutes
- following up any special issues that arise—at or between meetings
- keeping files and other records of the meeting agendas, minutes and supporting material
- following up actions from the meetings

If you are the Executive Officer, it is a good idea to spend some time with your Chairperson, to **make sure that there is a common understanding of your roles**. It is also useful to get to know the other members who attend the meeting.

It is particularly important to discuss both **what you can do** and **what is outside your role.**

Building understanding of, and respect for, each other's roles and responsibilities leads to good, productive meetings.

A well organized Executive Officer will have the following in place:
- **up to date** information about venues, especially their facilities, costs, booking procedures and contact details

- a **good filing system** that will contain the previous agendas and minutes, as well as any supporting material
- **details of meeting participants**, e.g. contact details and any special needs
- a **well planned schedule** of when tasks need to occur, especially:
  - deadlines for agenda items
  - distribution of the agenda,
  - preparation of the minutes,
  - and the lead time for booking of venues and facilities

When new members join the meeting, provide them with a package containing items such as:

- agendas and minutes from the past 2 or 3 meetings
- any documents about the purpose or scope of the meeting, such as a Terms of Reference or Meeting Brief
- details of deadlines for agenda items and supporting material
- a list of participant's responsibilities if you have one

A term as an Executive Officer is an excellent **personal development opportunity.** You will be exposed to a variety of chairing and general meeting skills have a chance to observe at close range the interactions of diverse groups, as well as listening to the content itself of the meetings. Seize the moment!

Participant's responsibilities

Every person who is part of a meeting bears some responsibility for the success of the meeting.

A good meeting needs a good Chairperson, an agenda, well organized minute taking and an appropriate venue—**and participants who contribute**! Like any activity, you will gain in proportion to how much you give.

If you are a 'switched on' meeting participant, you will:
- Be on time
- Be prepared: this includes bringing all the papers you need and being ready to report on your actions from the last meeting
- Come to the meeting prepared—read any papers distributed before the meeting
- Be assertive, but not aggressive, in the way you communicate

- Respect all members of the meeting; allow others to participate and don't talk over other people
- Stick to the topic
- Take your own notes—especially for tasks or actions that you will follow up
- Be flexible and open to other views
- Respect confidentiality
- If you don't understand something, ask for clarification
- Be prepared to participate in the discussions
- Be prepared to participate in the decision making
- Carry out the actions for which you accept responsibility, by the time you agree to do so

It's worth spending some time discussing and agreeing on a list of participant's responsibilities for your meetings. You can use this to regularly review your meeting conduct, and for new members to understand their role - it becomes '**the way we have meetings around here**'.

Minutes of a meeting

The Minutes of a meeting are the written record of the meeting—they provide information about the discussions, decisions and plans that have come from the meeting.

The style and format of the minutes of a *formal* meeting are determined by the rules and procedures governing the meeting. It is, however, very useful to also keep minutes of *informal* meetings.

Informal minutes can range from just a few points through to extensive notes.

Good minutes:
- are a brief but accurate record of the key points of the meeting
- record any decisions made at the meeting
- record who is responsible for any actions
- record who attended and who was absent
- follow the order of the agenda
- are written up and distributed quickly after the meeting

- are numbered and filed
- use a simple style of writing, and avoid discriminatory language

As you take the minutes, DO NOT write down everything that is said:

- **summarize**—get the key points only. You can practice this at other meetings you attend, or watching the news on TV, or a favorite TV program: it is a skill that only comes with practice!
- have a simple system that allows you to **identify who is speaking**—such as a table plan with their names—and then just write initials for who is speaking
- **speak to the chair** before the meeting and get agreement on how you will ask for clarification of anything
- **use a template** that allows you to quickly record dates and who is responsible for action on agenda items
- make sure you have everyone's **contact details**, such as emails
- if you need to **follow up** an item after the meeting, make sure you make the arrangements before the meeting ends...if you leave that until later you will end up wasting time chasing people
- make a time with the chair to **review your draft** of the meetings

- **don't panic**! It is okay to stop the meeting and ask for clarification

Some people use **a mind map** to take minutes. It is one of those simple yet very powerful tools that you can use for many purposes.

An excellent practice to develop is to **write and distribute the minutes very soon after the meeting**. The longer you leave writing up the minutes, then the easier it is to forget what was said—and what your notes mean.

In the same way, **the sooner you distribute the minutes,** then the more attention the attendees will give them, and the more likely they are to carry out the actions agreed at the meeting.

It is important to make sure that decisions and any **required actions are communicated clearly and accurately**—if nothing happens as a result of the meeting, then why did you bother to hold it or attend it?

It is a good practice to review the minutes of the previous meeting at the start of each new meeting. This has two powerful effects:
- people are quickly focused on the purpose of the meeting

- people get used to reporting on the achievement of the things they agreed to at the last meeting—**action** and **accountability**!

The Minute Taker's position is a vital one, and can be both frustrating and rewarding—this will largely depend on **how well organized** you are, and **how well you communicate with the Chairperson**.

There is an **example of some simple minutes**, and **a blank minute template** at the end of this tool.

The human dimension of the meeting: dealing with the people

People come to a meeting with many different needs as well as ways of behaving. Understanding some of what is motivating a person, and their preferences for behavior can be crucial in **improving the quality of your meetings.**

It is important to try to be objective and see every person at your meeting **as an individual** with their unique skills and abilities to contribute.

As a general principle, **people usually have a reason for their behavior that makes sense to them**—even if it appears unreasonable or unacceptable to you. Good communicators try to work with the individual—to open and then <u>keep open</u> the communication channels.

The **most productive meetings** happen when:

- people's preferences for behavior are recognized and valued
- there is a good mix of ALL the preferences
- people focus on behavior not personality

The task of a good chairperson—and of all participants—is to **listen actively, to listen with empathy, and to respond with respect.** Good communication comes when all present try to reflect on what is happening, looking at **behavior** not **personality** or **relationship**, and work with that.

There are always **options in communicating**—just because one person is behaving inappropriately does not mean that everyone else needs to behave in the same way.

A key to improving your meetings is to understand that people have **different preferences in the way they behave**—based on personality, experience and culture. The secret is to work <u>with</u> differences rather than seeing them as a nuisance or inappropriate.

A common difference that sometimes leads to misunderstanding is the emphasis a person may put on either the **task** or the **people.** For example, at one end of the scale there are those who are focused only on getting the task done, and at the other end, others who need to make sure that everyone is heard and acknowledged—on the 'process'.

A good meeting acknowledges that both aspects are important, and finds a balance where all are appropriately heard but at the same time, the job gets done.

Do you recognize any of the following **behavior patterns**—in yourself or in your colleagues?

- Some people who like detail and want to get on with the task
- Others who need to see the big picture and to see what might be next
- Some who like to make sure we finish what we've started before talking about the future
- Others who are interested in new ideas or possibilities
- Others who look for what won't work, while some who only see potential for success

Again, a good meeting will have a blend of each these behavior patterns—and if you don't have each one, then try asking a series of questions to make sure you have covered all aspects:

- Are we clear on the task? Do we have the key information?
- Have we checked the big picture—where does this fit in our planning?
- Are we ready to move on?
- Are we looking for new opportunities or new ways of doing things?
- Have we really checked out issues or problems? Have we missed any possibilities?

People also have different **preferences in how they learn**, and these affect the way they behave in meetings. Once you understand the learning preferences of each person at the meeting, you can make sure information and responses are given and asked for in ways that draw the best out of people.

The **learning styles** were first described by Honey & Mumford, and can be summarized as:

Theorists—what is the conceptual context. Theorists need the theory—the concepts and models—to think about before they can get into the content. "Tell me why we are might do something before you give me the details of what we might do" "Tell me how this fits in to the big picture".

Pragmatists—let me experiment with it. Pragmatists want to know how to apply things in the real world. "That is all very interesting, but does it apply in our work?"

Activist—how can I use it right now? Activists like to get moving, they like to try new things and have new experiences. "Can we stop discussing this and just get on and do it?" "This sounds interesting, let's try it"

Reflectors—let me think about this for a little while.

Reflectors prefer to watch others doing something before trying themselves and like to think about what they're doing. "Give me time to think about this idea quietly by myself, then I can comment or try it"

A good example of this is the person who is quiet in a meeting, yet often comes to you after a meeting with the comment or idea. It may be that their learning style is that a reflector. To get the best from these people in a meeting, give them time to think by asking other participants for their ideas first.

You may like to give this information about preferences to the people at your next meeting, and discuss how it might be used to improve your interactions.

There are many ways of describing these preferences, and a wide range of tests and quizzes that can help in clarifying these. Many of these are free—or quite inexpensive. Check out your local management or professional association, or your local library, or the Internet.

The **most productive meetings** happen when
- people's preferences for behavior are recognized and valued
- there is a good mix of ALL the preferences
- people focus on behavior not personality

People come to a meeting with many different needs as well as ways of behaving. Understanding some of what is motivating a person, and their preferences for behavior can be crucial in **improving the quality of your meetings.**

Distribute Checklist 5 to all participants as a good way to make sure that the strengths of the different preferences are drawn on, and to involve all the participants.

Make your meetings more productive. Use:

Checklist 5—getting the best out of people

A six step model for collaborative problem resolution

There are times when we all differ with the ideas, priorities, or statements of others—that is human nature! It is a good way for us to clarify and improve our own ideas. Difference is especially valuable because it often leads to new and better ways of doing things, and to learning on the part of all of us. But conflict can cause problems if not managed effectively.

We can experience difficulties in a meeting for many reasons. Some common ones are:

- **Miscommunication**: not listening well to each other, or misunderstanding what is said and what is meant
- **Confusion**: where goals or roles are not defined, or processes and procedures are not working—or workable
- **Differences in preferences**: the ways in which we see and describe the world

- **Personal needs**: when our everyday personal needs or interests are threatened

There are many different ways of handling differences, depending on issues such as:

- the culture of the group, organization and community
- the skills of the people involved
- the styles of communicating of the people involved—their preferences

Disagreements, differences or conflict can be healthy or they can be destructive—it all depends on how they are addressed. And how you address them is intimately connected with how your culture deals with them.

For some cultures, harmony and consensus are central; in others, individuality and independence are valued; while for yet others, the heritage and pride of the group, and loyalty to the leader are the highest priority.

Some people avoid conflict, others confront, while still others try to compromise or collaborate. **Collaboration is the most productive way of resolving differences—it may take a little longer but it has lasting results.**

There are some crucial principles in dealing with differences, disagreements and conflict:

- Demonstrate respect
- Understand yourself and your motivations and preferences
- Work at understanding the motivations and preferences of others
- Be prepared to look for the middle path
- Be positive
- Agree on standards about how you will work together

The first steps in dealing with difficulties and disagreements are:

- stop talking
- **listen** carefully
- **clarify** meanings
- find out what the other person is **feeling**
- consider **behavior** preferences
- **summarize** and reflect back what is being said
- look for common ground
- **avoid** demanding, criticizing and defending language
- use non-threatening, non-judgmental language

Use Checklist 6: Disagreements, differences and conflict

Conclusion

So, now you have it—the keys to 'Successful Meetings'.

We hope that you find the Checklists and Templates useful and that they help you to significantly improve the time and energy you spend in meetings.

We suggest that you reflect on your meetings regularly—we are often so caught up in everyday activities that we don't give ourselves permission to take time out to review, reflect and improve.

May your meetings are productive, successful and enjoyable!

Checklists, Examples and Templates

Please feel free to copy the Checklists, Examples and Templates and use them for your own meetings.

I ask, however, that you not copy the whole book. If you need more copies, please buy them. Thank you.

Checklist 1—Why hold this meeting?

1. Describe the meeting— when was it last held, who might attend, what arrangements have already been made?
2. Why are we having this meeting?
3. What do we want to happen as a result of holding this meeting?
4. Is there another way?
5. What other means of communicating or making a decision do we have?
6. Is a meeting the most cost effective way?
7. Who will have to pay the costs?
8. What would happen if we didn't hold the meeting?
9. Who would miss out?
10. What input would we overlook?

Checklist 2—Improving meetings

Think about the last two or three meetings that we have held, and consider these questions:

1. Which agenda items did we spend most time on?
2. What was the outcome from these?
3. Were we able to spend time on the most important items?
4. Was the expenditure of time and energy justified?
5. Which agenda items did we get most value from?
6. Are there any patterns of behaviour or decision making that can be identified? How can we build on or change them?

7. What changes could we make at the next

    meeting?

Checklist 3—Chairperson

1. **Find out who the participants will be**

   (What do you need to know about them?

   Do you need to be briefed by anyone?)

2. **Clarify the agenda, and your role**

   (Is your role one of an impartial

   chairperson, or do you need to contribute

   your views to the meeting?)

3. **Check out the venue**

   (If you have an Executive Officer, they

   may do this on your behalf).

4. **Decide whether you will start on time**

   (Will you (1) punish good time managers

   by making them wait for latecomers, or

   (2) reward poor time managers by waiting

   for them)?

5. **Prepare your opening remarks**

   (These may include: opening the meeting

   with a summary of the purpose of the

meeting, any comments about the agenda, and the anticipated time for the end of the meeting).

6. **Ask for any issues that people may have**

   (Is this your understanding of the meeting? Does anyone need to leave early? Is anyone representing someone else?)

7. **Ask questions often**

   (Both about the process and the task. Summarise regularly. Don't get side tracked).

8. **Be sensitive to cultural differences and needs**

9. **Make sure decisions are captured**

   (Make sure that the minutes or notes of the meeting are taken, and everyone is clear on what has been agreed—process as well as task)

10. **Clarify the time and venue of the next meeting**

(And when agenda items are required)

Checklist 4—Minute-taker

1. Identify at the start of the meeting who is taking the minutes, what is to be recorded, and how it is to be recorded.
2. Agree at the start of the meeting who will receive the minutes (participants or people outside the meeting).
3. Agree at the start of the meeting whether you are recording decisions or key points that were discussed. In either case, ask the chair to summarise frequently.
4. Clarify regularly what action is to be taken and by whom —it is not your role to either decide this or to follow up afterwards— your role is to write down the decisions of the meeting. (Follow up is the responsibility of the Chair, or another person nominated by the meeting).

5. It is quite appropriate for the minute taker to stop the chair or meeting and ask: 'what do you wish recorded?'
6. Minutes follow the agenda items.
7. Ideally, the minute taker should have no other role at the meeting.
8. Minutes provide agreement about an event so that people can act.
9. Minutes are a record of agreements, and the business, of the meeting.
10. Get the minutes out as quickly as possible after the meeting – the next day if possible. The longer you leave it, the harder the task becomes, and the less useful the minutes are.
11. We don't recommend tape recording a meeting for later writing up of minutes. It is inevitably a time consuming disaster!

Checklist 5—Getting the best out of people

Use this Checklist as a way of refocussing and redirecting discussion.

It gives people permission to look at all sides of an issue without getting stuck in old thinking patterns, personalities and previously held positions. It will also make sure your risk analysis is realistic and that more than one option is considered.

1.   **Why will it work?**

2.   **Why won't it work?**

3.   **Who else is involved?**

4.   **Who else cares about it?**

5.   **How have we defined success?**

6.   Have we considered all the details?

7.   What might be some other possibilities?

8.   What will be our next step, once we have left this meeting?

Checklist 6—Disagreements, differences and conflict

Step 1:

1. Decide—are we really willing to resolve the conflict?
2. If the answer is yes, then agree on how you will proceed—are you both willing to work with this model? Is there another model that we both might agree to use?
3. If the answer is n—what are the consequences? Where do we go to from here?
4. Can we do it by ourselves, or do we need an impartial facilitator?
5. Where and when are we going to meet?
6. Agree how you will speak—will you each take it in turns to talk, will there be a time limit, will you summarise what you have understood?

Step 2:

1. Clarify the problem or issue—clearly state what you each understand as the issue
2. Address the issue, not the person

3. Look for common areas—these may be common goals, common frustrations, common needs

Step 3:

1. Brainstorm some possible options—think creatively and identify a range of possible options. Try not to evaluate at this point
2. Once you have a range of options, now evaluate possibilities. If all these options are discounted, revisit the problem or issue to make sure you are clear on it, then try brainstorming some more options

Step 4:

1. Decide together on the best possible option
2. If there are several possibilities, prioritise them separately, then share your priorities and find out whether there is one that you can both accept

Step 5:

1. Agree on how you will put the option into place—what is your Action Plan?
2. Decide who will do what, when, how, how often and by when

Step 6:

1. Plan how you will evaluate the solution
2. What will you do if the option does not work?
3. Identify how you will evaluate what have we learned as a result of this process?

Checklist 7—Meetings start to finish

Use this Checklist when:
- you're just starting out, or
- to review the effectiveness of your meetings, or
- any time you want to improve your meetings

Why are we having this meeting?
Clarify the purpose of the meeting, is it to:
- share information
- give instructions
- make decisions
- generate ideas and options
- build the work team

What would happen if the meeting was not held? Is there a better way of addressing the issue than through a meeting?

Does the meeting need to be face to face, or could we use technology such as tele or video conferencing, or perhaps a webinar?

When should the meeting be held? Should the meeting be regularly scheduled?

Where will the meeting be held?

Who should attend and why? Does everyone need to stay for the whole meeting?

Who will chair the meeting? What will their role be? Is any training or coaching needed?

Who will be responsible for preparing and distributing the agenda? When and how will any supporting or background papers be circulated? Who will be responsible for taking, distributing and filing the minutes? Is any training or coaching needed?

What facilities are needed?
Consider:
- travelling time and parking
- seating and layout
- catering
- equipment such as whiteboards, projectors
- disabled access

How will we make decisions?

How will we add items to the agenda?

How will we manage latecomers?

How will we deal with conflict?

How will we check that the meeting has been effective?

Agenda Example

Wherever possible, the Agenda will be easier to read and work with if you use a table to format it. Below you will find two illustrations of a layout—one in text and the other using a table.

**Agenda for the Staff Meeting
to be held at 11 am to 12 noon, on Mon 31 Sep in the Lunch Room**

Item; Topic; Participation by/ Input from; Estimated Time

1. Present and Apologies; All; 2 mins
    Update from Director; Director; 5 mins
    Proposed new product launch; Marketing Manager; 15 mins. This item could show details such as:
    - description of product including price, benefits, differentiation from previous products, etc
    - when
    - where
    - staff involvement, including training
    - any system changes
    - questions
2. Update on Sales figures; Sales Manager; 3 mins

3. Occupational Health Safety & Welfare; OHS&W Rep; 3 mins
   - This item could show details such as any lost time through accidents or any required training
4. Housekeeping Keeping the lunchroom tidy; Office Manager All; 3 mins
5. Any other business; All; 10 mins
   (This item makes time for staff to raise urgent or important items for discussion. Once people are accustomed to sending agenda items to the meeting convenor, the time allocated to this item should decrease)
6. Next meeting; Director; 2 mins

The same Agenda laid out in a table:

Agenda for the Staff Meeting to be held at 11 am to 12 noon, on Mon 31 Sep in the Lunch Room			
Item	Topic	Participation by/ Input from	Estimated Time
1	Present/Apologies	All	2 mins
2	Update from Director	Director	5 mins

3	Proposed new product launch. *This item could show details such as:* • description of product including price, benefits, differentiation from previous products, etc) • when • where • staff involvement, including training • any system changes • questions	Marketing Manager	15 mins
4	Update on Sales figures	Sales Manager	3 mins
5	Occupational Health Safety & Welfare *This item could show details such as any lost time through accidents or any required training*	OHS&W Rep	

6	Housekeeping - Keeping the lunchroom tidy	Office Manager All	3 mins
7	Any other business *(This item makes time for staff to raise urgent or important items for discussion. Once people are accustomed to sending agenda items to the meeting convenor, the time allocated to this item should decrease)*	All	10 mins
8	Next meeting	Director	2 mins

Agenda Template

Agenda for the
_____ Meeting
to be held at _____ to _____ on _____
in _____

Item	Topic	Participation by/ Input from	Est Time

Example of Minutes

Wherever possible, the Minutes will be easier to read and work with if you use a table to format it. Below you will find two illustrations of a layout—one in text and the other using a table.

Minutes of the Staff Meeting held at 11 am on Mon 30 Sep in the Lunch Room
Item; Topic; Action
1; Present & Apologies; Managers

> Present: J Smith, E Broem, T Lee, A Singh, T Dobroski, F Green, G Verdi, O Phoster, L Sims, L Tomas, N Waugh, R Taylor
> Apologies: C Robin, P Keffner

Item; Topic; Action
2; Key points from Director: All staff

Key Points
- all staff need to watch for possible wastage from the new packaging process
- the computer system upgrade is now complete, and the pricing package is working well

- sales figures for the past quarter have been excellent
- suggestions are requested about the possible disposal of the old packaging equipment. There will be a bonus for ideas that help recoup some money

Item; Topic; Action
3; R Taylor (Marketing); Managers to let R Taylor know who will be attending, by Tues 2 pm.

R Taylor gave the details of the new product (see attached notes). All staff are to attend familiarisation sessions next Wed and Thurs afternoons.

Item; Topic; Action
4; Sales Figures; L Thomas & All Staff

The Sales figures for the last 2 months are excellent (see attached notes). The two green lines of product (no BX11 and BX 12a) are the only ones not meeting sales projections, and there will be a big promotion for these later this month. Any suggestions should be given to L Tomas (Sales) by next Mon.

Item; Topic; Action
5; OHS&W; Managers, All staff

This month there was one work injury reported, cause: not following safe lifting procedure. The 'Safe

Lifting Procedures' brochure was handed out to all staff as a reminder. Managers are to check that all staff have done the basic OHS&W courses.

Item; Topic; Action
6; Lunch Room; All staff
All staff are reminded that it is their individual responsibility to keep the lunch room tidy.

Item; Topic; Action
7; Next Meeting; All Staff

Next meeting will be held on Wed 30 Oct, at 11 am, in the lunch room.

On the following page, you will find the same Minutes, but in table format.

Minutes of the Staff Meeting held at 11 am on Mon 30 Sep 2004 in the Lunch Room		
Item	**Topic**	**Action**
1	Present: J Smith, E Broem, T Lee, A Singh, T Dobroski, F Green, G Verdi, O Phoster, L Sims, L Tomas, N Waugh, R Taylor Apologies: C Robin, P Keffner	Managers
2	Key points from Director: • all staff need to watch for possible wastage from the new packaging process • the computer system upgrade is now complete, and the pricing package is working well • sales figures for the past quarter have been excellent • suggestions are requested about the possible disposal of the old packaging equipment. There will be a bonus for ideas that help recoup some money	All staff

	Minutes...continued	
3	R Taylor (Marketing) gave the details of the new product (see attached notes). All staff are to attend familiarisation sessions next Wed and Thurs afternoons.	Managers to let R Taylor know who will be attending, by Tues 2 pm.
4	The Sales figures for the last 2 months are excellent (see attached notes). The two green lines of product (no BX11 and BX 12a) are the only ones not meeting sales projections, and there will be a big promotion for these later this month. Any suggestions should be given to L Tomas (Sales) by next Mon.	L Tomas (Sales) All staff
5	This month there was one work injury reported, cause: not following safe lifting procedure. The 'Safe Lifting Procedures' brochure was handed out to all staff as a reminder. Managers are to check that all staff have done the basic OHS&W courses.	Managers All staff
6	All staff are reminded that it is their individual responsibility to keep the lunch room tidy.	All staff
7	Next meeting will be held on Wed 30 Oct, at 11 am, in the lunch room.	All staff

Minutes of the_____Meeting held at _____on _____ in/at_____		
Item	Topic	Action
1	Present:	
2		
3		
4		
5	Next meeting will be held on_____ at _____ in/at_____	

Author Profile

J H Hood has a Bachelor of Arts, a Diploma in Education and the National Medal. She has extensive experience across government, the private sector and community organizations: as a senior manager as well as training adults in the workplace in a wide range of management and personal skills.

She has worked with many thousands of people, helping them to build the skills to survive and thrive in the workplace. Feedback on her training and coaching focuses on how practical her material is, and how quickly positive outcomes come from using it.

The 'How To" series comes form her love of writing and her experience helping people build their skills and knowledge.

She and her partner live in the foothills of Adelaide, where they can watch koalas climbing the tree outside her study window. Their two cats don't even stir!

The delightful graphics are by Mal Briggs: http://www.impactcomics.com.au

Look out for more books in J H Hood's "How To series.

Available now on Amazon:
"How to Book of Writing Skills: Words at Work"

36647897R00044

Made in the USA
Lexington, KY
29 October 2014